Original title:
Aloe There, Sweetheart

Copyright © 2025 Creative Arts Management OÜ
All rights reserved.

Author: Seraphina Caldwell
ISBN HARDBACK: 978-1-80581-815-1
ISBN PAPERBACK: 978-1-80581-342-2
ISBN EBOOK: 978-1-80581-815-1

Bursting with Affection Beneath the Leaves

In the garden, love does sprout,
A plant so lovely, there's no doubt.
With spiky arms and plenty of cheer,
It hugs you close, then disappears!

Flourish of Heart and Soil

A pot of dreams sits on the shelf,
It whispers sweetly, 'Date yourself!'
With every sip from morning tea,
Plants giggle softly, just wait and see.

The Quiet Elegance of Green Love

In layers of soil, secrets dwell,
As plants conspire, casting their spell.
With every bloom, a chuckle grows,
Nature's humor, nobody knows!

Rooted in Soft Affection

Underneath the moonlit sky,
The greens exchange a bashful sigh.
With roots entwined, they dance and sway,
In this quirky love, they'll always stay!

Tender Vows Under Spiny Arms

In a garden lush with prickly kin,
We swear our love will never thin.
With thorns to hug and leaves to sway,
Let's promise laughter every day.

Our hearts entwined like tangled vines,
With quirky quirks that spark our signs.
We'll dance among the sunlit green,
In jokes and jabs, the joy's unseen.

Love That Blossoms in the Sun

Beneath the rays of golden light,
Our humor blooms, oh what a sight!
With sunny smiles and silly pranks,
We cherish giggles, give our thanks.

Each bloom a laugh, each petal, glee,
In nature's playground, wild and free.
We sip the nectar, sweet and bold,
Our silly stories forever told.

Nurtured by Nature's Touch

Your laughter grows like greenest leaves,
A quirky charm that never leaves.
With nature's hands and playful grace,
We find our joy in every place.

A garden maze of jokes and cheer,
We wander through with no one near.
With hints of spice in every breath,
We blossom boldly, defy all death.

Serenity in Every Leaf

In every leaf, a chuckle waits,
A calm that dances, never sedates.
With thoughts as light as air we share,
In silly moments, nothing compares.

Our hearts aglow, like stars that shine,
We find the joy in every line.
So here's to love, both bright and sweet,
In nature's arms, our lives complete.

Embrace in the Desert Heat

In the desert sun, we dance and sway,
With shades of green, our worries drift away.
You steal a sip from my quirky mug,
While cacti giggle, they just give a shrug.

A tumbleweed rolls, a laugh on its run,
We chase after giggles, always having fun.
Your laughter's the shade from the blazing light,
Together we bloom, in joy so bright.

Love Among the Potted Leaves

In pots we sit, a leafy brigade,
Whispering secrets, no reason to fade.
You water my heart with a splash of cheer,
While I sunbathe, wishing you were near.

A squirrel peeks in, joining our crew,
We're all just plants, kooky but true.
With blossoms so silly, we giggle and sway,
In this botanical ballet, we play.

Heart's Bloom in the Sunlight

Our hearts are petals, opened wide,
Under the sunlight, together we bide.
A bee tries to woo, but we laugh and tease,
As we stretch our limbs in a gentle breeze.

With silly faces, we chase the flies,
As butterflies twirl with joyful sighs.
Nature's a stage, with us in the show,
With every petal, our love starts to grow.

Soothing Touch of Nature's Heart

Your touch is soothing, like gentle rain,
Beneath the shade where time's hardly a chain.
We trade playful quips, while ferns softly sigh,
As a ladybug lands, giving us a high.

We've got roots entangled in this fun game,
In this garden of laughter, we've made our name.
As blossoms erupt, in colors so bright,
We giggle together, from morning to night.

Embracing Nature's Tender Touch

In a garden where greens hold sway,
A little plant peeks out to play.
It shakes its arms in a lively dance,
While bees take part in a buzzing prance.

With spiky tips that seem quite bold,
It warms the heart without the cold.
In sunlit laughs, it soaks up cheer,
A prickly plant, but we still hold dear.

Reach for Love Among the Thorns

Amidst the blooms, a story grows,
Of gentle hearts that nobody knows.
With every poke, they laugh and squeal,
Finding joy in the playful peel.

If love can flourish in spiky frames,
Then surely, darling, this is our game.
Each thorn a warning we choose to ignore,
Together we thrive, seeking more and more.

The Symmetry of Heart and Leaf

Two hearts like leaves in playful twirl,
One soft and sweet, the other a whirl.
With patterns that twist and sprout anew,
A classic blend of green and blue.

In every crease, a secret resides,
Where laughter hides, and love abides.
Like leaves entwined in a gentle breeze,
We dance around, intent to please.

Whimsical Leaves and Love's Secrets

In leafy whispers, secrets are found,
Where giggles echo all around.
With playful nods, the branches sway,
Creating mischief in shades of gray.

The roots below grow deep and wide,
While leafy fun takes us for a ride.
So here we stand, with hearts aglow,
In nature's arms, we'll steal the show.

Garden of Gentle Affections

In a garden bright and full of cheer,
Plants gossip softly, lend an ear.
The cacti chuckle, with quirks so fine,
While daisies wink, 'Oh, she's so divine!'

Marigolds dance, beckoning the bees,
The roses blush, swaying in the breeze.
Joking with shadows, the herbs play tricks,
As laughter echoes, a joy that sticks.

A Soft Embrace of Foliage

Leaves whisper secrets on the vine,
One leaf says, 'Darling, you're simply divine!'
The ferns all giggle, their fronds in a twist,
'Who needs a spa when you have this mist?'

In this plush realm where the sunbeams dance,
Even the weeds join in the romance.
Crickets chirp, adding to the tune,
With butterflies thinking, 'We're all on a swoon!'

Sweetness Found in Prickly Places

A plucky plant with spikes so bold,
Hosts parties where laughter unfolds.
Each thorn a tickle, each bloom a tease,
Flirting with bugs in the warm summer breeze.

'Hey, prickly friend! You're quite the charmer!'
A petal answers, 'I'm no farmer!
But who can resist these juicy delights?
Let's party until we see starry nights!'

Serenade of the Succulent Soul

In a pot on the shelf, a heart beats bright,
With succulent dreams that glow through the night.
'Oh, squeeze me tight!' the jade plant calls,
'Our love's like sunshine; it never falls!'

With laughter and joy from the herbs nearby,
Puns burst forth like a sparkling sky.
'Let's toast to the roots that dance underground,
In this quirky love, true joy can be found!'

Heartbeats Underneath the Canopy

Under leaves so thick and lush,
Your giggles blend with the rush.
Squirrels dance, they think they're cool,
While we play our silly fool.

Sunshine peeks through branches wide,
You chase me, oh what a ride!
With every twist, we both just laugh,
Two crazy hearts on a leafy path.

Dancing in the Garden of Affinity

In blooms so bright, we frolic free,
Your smile beams, a sight to see.
Butterflies kiss our silly hats,
While bees think we're all just chitchats.

Twirling weeds, we drop and roll,
Each petal feels like purest gold.
In this dance of laugh and jest,
We find our hearts are truly blessed.

The Allure of Emerald Enchantment

Green vines twist, an emerald spell,
You can't stop laughing; oh, so well!
Tangled branches above us sway,
As you say, 'Let's dance all day!'

The little frogs let out a cheer,
For our frolicking has no fear.
With each giggle, the world feels right,
Caught in glee, from day to night.

Loving You Through the Seasons

In springtime's bloom, the flowers tease,
You trip on petals, land with ease.
Summer brings us lazy daze,
And silly games that last for days.

When autumn leaves begin to fall,
We jump and laugh; it's our free-for-all.
Winter hugs us with its chill,
But together, warmth is what we feel.

Resilient Love Through the Seasons

In winter's chill, we laugh and play,
Our love grows warm, come what may.
With springtime blooms, we dance around,
Even plants know love is profound.

Summer's heat, we sip on tea,
Aisles of sunshine, you and me.
Autumn leaves, they whirl and twirl,
As we both spin, just like this world.

Serenade of Succulent Souls

In sunlit banks we share a drink,
With every sip, the silly sync.
A cactus grin, a prickly jest,
You've daftly passed the silly test.

With succulent hugs, we trade our quips,
No need for signs or fancy scripts.
A wink and laugh, our roots entwined,
In laughter's bloom, true love's designed.

Twisted Vows

We made our vows, all silly rhymes,
To dance through life like tangled vines.
You said 'I do', with cupcake crumbs,
While I just smiled, amidst the puns.

In messy kitchens, we create,
Our recipes just can't wait.
With laughter served on every plate,
Our twisted love is truly great.

Gentle Growth

We started small, a tiny sprout,
With laughs so loud, they leave no doubt.
As time goes by, we stretch and bend,
Our gentle growth, we can defend.

Through sunny days and moonlit nights,
We sprout new dreams and silly fights.
With every smile, our roots go deep,
In laughter's soil, our hearts we'll keep.

Lush Affection Under the Sun

Beneath the rays, we bask in fun,
Our love feels fresh, just like the sun.
We chase the shade, both quick and sly,
In joy we bloom, like plants nearby.

With every sunbeam, a funny tale,
Through garden paths, we laugh and trail.
Our hearts connect like leaves in breeze,
In lush affection, we do as we please.

Unraveling Vines of Togetherness

Twisting and turning, we laugh with glee,
In this green jungle, just you and me.
Foolish plants whisper secrets in the sun,
Together we dance, our hearts weigh a ton.

Garden gloves on, we dig and we play,
Planting our dreams in a comical ballet.
Worms wiggling under, trying to steal the show,
Yet in our joyful chaos, we steal the glow.

Tended Touches and Soft Leaves

Your hand in mine, we prune with delight,
Snipping away at the weeds in our sight.
We laugh at the bugs, those critters so bold,
In our leafy romance, a story unfolds.

Soft petals brush past, a tickle, a tease,
Nature's giggles float gently on the breeze.
With every small bloom, a chuckle erupts,
In the garden of warmth, whimsy disrupts.

A Garden of Unspoken Words

In silence we share a flower-filled glance,
A language of blooms, a raucous romance.
The daisies roll over, gossiping bright,
While we laugh at the sun, in splendid light.

Beneath tangled vines, we plot our next scheme,
With puns in the petals, we weave a sweet dream.
The roses are blushing, our secrets out loud,
With laughter entwined, we're absurdly proud.

Nature's Interlude of Love

Here in this paradise, we sow seeds of fun,
Sipping sweet nectar under the warm sun.
The bees buzz around, with a comedic sting,
And every small flower feels like a king.

We sing to the cacti, so prickly and shy,
While chortling at ferns that seem to sigh.
In nature's embrace, we frolic and twine,
Two silly souls lost in a wild design.

The Gentle Heart of a Plant

In my garden, there's a friend,
With spiky armor that won't bend.
A soft heart within a tough disguise,
Witty banter, oh how time flies!

It doesn't gossip, doesn't pout,
Just stands there, ever keen to sprout.
Tells me secrets in the breeze,
Like how to chill and just be at ease.

Oh, the laughter it does bring,
Whispering tales of springtime fling.
Together we share sunlight's grace,
To embrace life at a slower pace.

So here's to you, my leafy mate,
You make my heart so light and straight.
Let's giggle through our leafy age,
For love blooms best on nature's stage.

Love Wrapped in Spiky Leaves

Nestled snug in a sunny nook,
Mystery wrapped in a funky crook.
Not just a plant, but a quirky friend,
Banter blossoms that never end.

When I'm feeling down or blue,
You crack a smile — it's true!
Brushing my worries away with ease,
Together we dance in the fragrant breeze.

You prickle but never bite,
Always there to make it right.
In your company, I can thrive,
With humor keeping us alive.

Let's raise a toast, dear green delight,
To wacky moments, day and night.
With laughter sprouting like springtime rain,
Our love blooms deeply, free from pain.

Warmth of the Living Green

In bright sunlight, you lean and sway,
With each petal, you steal my day.
A chuckle shared under leafy shade,
Your spiky smile never will fade.

Oh, the joy you bring, my little mate,
Together we jest and celebrate.
Grinning from your pot with glee,
You hold my heart, it's plain to see.

With rhythms of nature, we chuckle loud,
Rooted firmly in a vibrant crowd.
But still, my dear, you stand alone,
A green companion made of stone.

Frolic through the garden, let's pretend,
That laughter's the message we always send.
In this wild life, where humor's king,
Here's to love in every little fling.

Heartstrings in a Pot

In a corner by the window's light,
You flourish so tall, it's quite a sight.
With each quirk and every twist,
You transform every gloom into bliss.

Your leaves, a tapestry of grace,
Wrapped in charm, they set the pace.
I share my tales, you just sit and grin,
A friendship cemented beneath my skin.

Dance with me in the sunny glow,
Your spiky hugs are what I know.
In this garden of shared delight,
We bloom together, hearts so light.

So here's a wink to the days ahead,
To silly moments and laughter spread.
With heartstrings tied, we'll never part,
For you're the joy that fills my heart.

Serenity Among Spines

In the garden where we play,
Spiky friends come out to sway.
Witty banter, laughter so bright,
Guarded by spines, yet hearts take flight.

Cactuses wear a prickly crown,
But their humor brings no frown.
With each giggle, we all survive,
In this patch where joy's alive.

Among the thorns, our jokes we toss,
Like petals in a playful gloss.
Each jest a balm for every sting,
In this green space, we're the kings.

So let's toast to these leafy pals,
With spiky hugs and laughter yells.
In serenity, we find our way,
As joy blooms fresh with every day.

Flourishing Bonds in Fertile Grounds

In soil rich with laughter's cheer,
We plant our roots, our dreams so clear.
With each sprout, a tale unfolds,
Of blossomed love in greens and golds.

We dance with daisies, twirl with thyme,
Making mischief, savoring time.
Geranium smiles that never fade,
In our patch, sweet memories made.

Beneath the sunlight, puns take flight,
As creatures giggle through the night.
Caring whispers, jokes to sprout,
In these gardens, love's what it's about.

We gather blooms, a playful bunch,
Sharing stories over lunch.
In fertile grounds, our hearts expand,
With roots entwined, hand in hand.

Hearts that Thrive in Warmth

Under the sun's warm, golden glow,
We cherish moments, letting love flow.
Every smile like petals unfurled,
In the meadow, our joy is twirled.

While shadows creep, we won't retreat,
For with humor, we're never beat.
In every giggle, we find our place,
Rooted together, we embrace.

The warmth of laughter lights the way,
As silly pranks lead us astray.
In this riot of greens, we navigate,
Where hearts unite and celebrate.

Each shared glance is a treasure found,
Among the blooms, our hopes abound.
In this garden, no heart can grieve,
For joy and warmth are what we weave.

The Language of Green Love

In leafy whispers, secrets throng,
Where every joke feels right and wrong.
We speak in laughter, never shy,
Among the greens, our hearts reply.

With every chuckle, roots entwine,
Creating bonds that brightly shine.
A playful tease or gentle nudge,
Turns the garden into a flood.

Let's roll in petals, skip in grass,
In this language, we'll not pass.
For each flower tells a tale,
Of love we nurture, never pale.

So here's a toast, we'll raise our hands,
To the green love that understands.
In every leaf, our joy is found,
A garden's magic, laughter's sound.

Playful Tenderness in Nature's Arms

In a patch of sunny dreams, they twirl,
The leaves dance, giving the world a whirl.
Cactus tries to join, but oh, so prickly,
Laughter erupts, ever so quickly.

Bumbles in bloom with giggles aflutter,
A butterfly giggles, searching for butter.
The bees wear tiny hats, oh so funny,
Pollinating jokes, sweet as honey.

Squirrels play tag with pinecones galore,
Squeaks and chirps make a wild encore.
Underneath the laughter, roots entwine,
Holding a secret, a love divine.

Nature's arms rock crickets to sleep,
While giggles echo, promises to keep.
In the garden where laughter prevails,
Tenderness blooms as chaos entails.

Nurtured by Love's Light

Under the sun's cheeky gaze,
Giggles tumble in sunlight's rays.
A daisy pretends it's a dancing star,
While dandelions dream of going far.

Worms don spectacles, so refined,
Wiggling with style, truly one of a kind.
The soil chuckles, gently embracing,
Life's funny waltz, with nature pacing.

Love sprouts wildly, roots intertwined,
Feeling the warmth, sweet and unconfined.
Chasing shadows with a wink and a twist,
In the glow of laughter, none can resist.

The garden smiles in hues bright and bold,
Whispers of secrets, stories untold.
Nurtured by joy, this playful right,
Blooming by day, enchanted by night.

The Pulse of Leafy Hearts

In the heart of the meadow, a giggle takes flight,
With leaflets and petals bouncing, oh, what a sight!
Each heartbeat of nature plays a sweet tune,
As the sky chuckles with a gleaming monsoon.

Roots tickle the earth, a game of surprise,
Each droplet of dew twinkles, brightening eyes.
Whispers of wind spin yarns of delight,
Nature's pulse dances, oh, what a height!

Frogs in top hats croak out a jest,
While ants march on, all dressed to impress.
The sun glares down, trying not to frown,
At the hilarity blooming all over town.

In this leafy haven where smiles ignite,
Love's funny flair makes everything right.
With hearts made of chlorophyll, pulsed with glee,
Nature's comedy unfolds endlessly.

Knots of Green and Warmth

Tangled vines create their own joke,
A leafy magician makes rabbits evoke.
As the daisies giggle with petals in tow,
The laughter of greens begin to flow.

The branches gossip, sharing sweet tales,
Of bumbles and fumbles and curious snails.
Each knot of green whispers secrets so dear,
In a chorus of chuckles that everyone hears.

With warmth of the sun, a prankster shines bright,
Playing tricks on shadows, igniting delight.
The grass tickles toes while laughter erupts,
Nature's own banquet where joy interrupts.

Around playful roots, love jumps and winks,
As swaying blooms tea party and thinks.
In this garden where humor takes stage,
Knots of green cradle hearts, joy is the wage.

When Leaves Dance in the Breeze

Leaves twirl and spin, a leafy ballet,
Squirrels giggle as they join in the play.
Birds chirp their laughter, a feathery crowd,
Nature's own comedy—it's funny and loud.

Wind tickles branches, they sway side to side,
Plants gossip softly, where secrets reside.
A flower winks slyly, its petals a-peek,
Nature's courtroom of jesters, no one's too meek.

Sunshine pops in, bringing warmth and delight,
While shadows drop jokes, a comical sight.
The grass wears a grin, a vibrant green hue,
In this playful garden, there's laughter anew.

Here joy spills over, in greens bright and bold,
Life's little stories, in petals retold.
With each step we take, absurdities rise,
In this jolly place, we find love and sighs.

Bask in Nature's Tender Glow

The sun's soft embrace, a warm hug of light,
Even the daffodils dance in sheer delight.
And bees in their buzz, gossip wildly on flight,
It's a laughing affair, such a splendid sight.

Butterflies flutter, in costumes so grand,
They trip on their wings, oh isn't it planned?
With petals as cushions, they land with such flair,
Each landing a tumble, they laugh in the air.

The trees stand like giants, chuckling so low,
As ants march in line, their tiny parade show.
Every rustle and croak, echoes a joke,
Nature's a comedian, laughter bespoke.

Basking in warmth, with friends near and far,
We dance in the glow, like a shooting star.
So raise up your glass to this wonderful scene,
In the heart of the wild, we laugh and we glean.

Cherished Moments Among the Greens

In the meadow of smiles, with daisies so sweet,
We gather our giggles, in nature's heartbeat.
The grass whispers stories, the clouds hover near,
Holding hands with joy, we banish all fear.

A turtle reflects, with wisdom so sly,
While frogs croak a symphony beneath the blue sky.
Each moment we capture, with laughter and cheer,
Nature winks at us, come gather, come near.

Giggling together, we share silly tales,
As shadows stretch long, and the daylight fails.
The stars begin twinkling, a celestial jest,
In this lush greenery, we giggle the best.

So here's to the merriment, the green and the gold,
To all of the stories that nature has told.
Let's toast to the moments that make us feel bright,
With laughter and love, in the soft evening light.

Sweetness of the Earth's Embrace

Oh, to wander where flowers poke fun at the bees,
And moss cushions laughter, a soft, leafy tease.
When the sun dips low with a wink and a nod,
Even rocks break a smile, on this earth they applaud.

The ripe berries chuckle, with sweetness they burst,
Each bite's a small giggle, our taste buds immersed.
The roots hold their secrets, in whispers they share,
Nature's quirks abound, in this love-filled air.

Wild mint in the breeze gives us tickles and grins,
As crickets crack jokes, where the laughter begins.
Upon our adventures, in meadows of cheer,
Every nook's filled with joy; it's perfectly clear.

So let's dance on the grass, where the night meets the day,
With fireflies winking, leading us on the way.
In the arms of the earth, we embrace all its grace,
With giggles and fun, our hearts race in this space.

Sweet Promises in Bloom

In a pot with sunshine bright,
I promised you pure delight.
You watered me with jokes and glee,
Now I'm thriving, can't you see?

With every sprout, a giggle grows,
You'll find me in your silly clothes.
I'll bloom in colors, bold and bright,
Make every day a funny sight.

Though I might be a little prickly,
Your laughter makes my heart so sickly.
Bring on the jokes, let's not be coy,
With every poke, you bring me joy!

So here we are, my leafy friend,
Sprouting love that will not end.
With you beside, I can't complain,
In laughter's shade, we both will reign.

Affectionate Roots in Sandy Soil

In sandy soil where we both dwell,
Our roots entwined, what a sweet spell.
You call me quirky, what a surprise,
But my heart blooms, just like the skies.

We dance with winds that make us sway,
In our garden, come what may.
With every grain, our love does mix,
Amidst our laughter, the perfect fix.

February brought us silly hearts,
Who knew affection grew in parts?
Let's giggle 'til our sides are sore,
In this sandy patch, I want you more!

With roots so deep, and fun in sight,
We'll shine together, oh what a sight!
We'll whisper jokes among the blooms,
Creating joy that fills the rooms.

Love in the Shade of Foliage

Under the cover of leafy green,
We share sweet secrets, a tranquil scene.
In nature's arms, we laugh and tease,
Like playful kids, we do what we please.

With every rustle, a new joke flows,
In this green haven, affection grows.
Your smile shines brighter than the sun,
With you around, we only have fun.

The leaves may hide our silly ways,
But within our hearts, it's a sunny blaze.
With whispers shared in playful tone,
In this leafy space, I feel at home.

So let's embrace this foliage spree,
In every giggle, there's you and me.
With shadows dancing, let's not rush,
In laughter's arms, our spirits hush.

Prickles and Petals of Affection

In a garden full of prickly jest,
Love blooms in petals, oh what a quest!
Though slight surprises may pain my skin,
Your laughter's the prize that makes me grin.

You tickle my heart like a gentle breeze,
While we share puns beneath the trees.
With every thorn, a story untold,
In our patch of humor, watch it unfold.

Blooming bright with each silly fray,
Our love's a dance, come out and play!
In color and laughter, we'll find our way,
With prickles and petals, we'll seize the day.

So here we are, my spiky delight,
In this garden, everything's right.
With laughter and love, we'll surely thrive,
Together forever, oh how we'll strive!

Garden Paths of Kindred Spirits

In a garden where laughter blooms,
We stumble through each other's rooms.
You tripped on a pot, and so did I,
Laughter echoes under the sky.

With plant jokes that we often share,
Like how cacti never need a care.
Your plant's in the corner, looking quite wise,
But it's thriving on all your good lies.

We dance with the weeds, a charming affair,
While pollinators buzz, without a care.
You say I'm a rose, prickly at times,
But you're the dandelion of nicked-up rhymes.

Together we bumble, a beautiful sight,
Through tangled vines in the soft moonlight.
You sprinkle the soil with giggles untamed,
In this garden of mischief, we're both unashamed.

Healing Hues of Togetherness

In colors that blend, we find our place,
A canvas of giggles, an artful embrace.
You're blue like the sky, I'm green as the grass,
Together we make quite the colorful class.

With paint on our hands and dirt on our shoes,
We mix up emotions, we'll never lose.
You laugh at my puns — or maybe just sigh,
But I know deep down, you're glad I'm nearby.

We splash life with hues that no one can miss,
Emotional rainbows, in a sea of bliss.
When thick clouds roll in and the rain starts to fall,
We just pull out the umbrellas, we're ready for all.

Through every storm, our palette stays bright,
With laughter and warmth, we'll paint the night.
Healing together, in vibrant delight,
Our friendship's a masterpiece, a sparkling light.

Tender Succulents at Dusk

In our garden, the sun takes a bow,
As succulent whispers fill up the how.
You tell me your secrets, they're all sugar sweet,
While my cactus pricks your toes, can't take a seat.

At dusk, we unwind with puns and some flair,
We joke that the plants are divas, I swear.
You brush off the leaves, I flick off the bugs,
Our laughter, a melody, full of snug hugs.

With soft hues of green, our spirits entwine,
As we sip our cool drinks, in this moment divine.
What's with the cactus? It wants to steal show!
But we're the stars here, don't you know?

Caress of Green Whispers

In moonlight's touch, we laugh like a breeze,
Among leafy vines, our hearts find their ease.
You trip over roots, oh what a sight,
But I cradle your laughter, hold it tight.

Whispers of green in our secret glade,
We trade tiny jokes, in the twilight parade.
You claim you're a fern, regal and grand,
While I'm in disguise, just a weed on the land.

We twirl in the shadows, a quirky duet,
Among leafy companions, we're never upset.
Caressed by the night, in joy we reside,
Among our green whispers, side by side.

A Potted Romance

In a pot, where dreams reside,
A leafy heart sits side by side.
With soil and sun, they play a game,
While each whispers a funny name.

A cactus claims it knows the score,
While a fern tries to dance on the floor.
But everyone knows it's just a ruse,
As they laugh at their own green muse.

The blooms in pastel, a cheerful sight,
Chatting away beneath the light.
"Look at me!" one flower beams,
"I'm the star of all the plant-based dreams!"

Yet as the gardener strolls on through,
They start a battle—who's more blue?
But in the end, it's love they find,
In each silly leaf, twined and aligned.

Whispers in the Greenhouse

In the greenhouse, secrets fly,
Petals gossip, not shy, oh my!
"Did you see the new sprout's hair?"
Chirped a violet with a flair.

The ivy rolled its leafy eyes,
Said, "I'm off to catch some lies!"
A joke about weeds went round the place,
While succulents smiled with spiky grace.

A fern waved at a timid bud,
"Here's a tip: just don't get mud!"
Potted hearts in sunlight bask,
Bursting with humor's sweet task.

"Let's have a dance," a flower said,
They twirled around, love widespread.
In this cozy plot, laughter shimmers,
As potted souls find joy that glimmers.

Finding Love in the Garden's Shadows

In the shadows, where couples bloom,
A daisy waits, filling the room.
"I'll take your petals to the ball,"
Said a tulip, trying not to fall.

Against the fence, a stubborn vine,
Attempts to snag a flirt, divine.
"Hey, don't leaf me," it sweetly cried,
But the rose just rolled her eyes wide.

Here, romance grows in silly ways,
With puns that brighten cloudy days.
A gopher spies, and lets out a chuckle,
As flowers in love engage in a struggle.

With laughter echoing through the land,
Two daisies clasped a tiny hand.
Amidst the lettuce and leafy pride,
They giggled together, side by side.

Serenade of Succulents

In the desert of pots, they meet, oh dear,
A duo of succulents, quips, and cheer.
"Let's sing a tune of prickly delight,"
Said one to the other, under twilight.

With each twist and turn, they spin and sway,
"Is it just me, or is it plant date day?"
A joke about roots made them both chortle,
As laughter danced in their little huddle.

Along the windowsill, dreams take flight,
"Who knew we'd be the stars tonight?"
Their leaves shimmered like stars above,
In the green realm, they found their love.

A wink, a nudge, a playful tease,
Succulent hearts don't aim to please.
Together they flourish, a comical pair,
In their garden of fun, not a single care.

Tender Leaves of Affection

In a pot so round and small,
A plant that thinks it's ten feet tall.
With spiky spikes and a wink,
It gives my heart a gentle clink.

I water it with love and care,
But it stares back, as if to dare.
To steal my sunshine, what a sneak!
It's sassy, green, and oh so chic.

When friends come by, they laugh and tease,
I tell them, "Don't pull at those leaves!"
Its style shines, a top-notch flair,
With personality that's quite rare.

So here's to you, my leafy mate,
You never make me feel out of date.
A quirky charm that's hard to beat,
You root for me, my heart's sweet treat.

Succulent Whispers in the Breeze

A plant that's chubby, full of sparks,
In sunny corners, it leaves its marks.
Whispers float on gentle air,
Telling tales of succulent care.

Oh, how it giggles when I'm near,
With leaves that dance, it shows no fear.
In laughter, we grow, side by side,
Its prickly hugs, my heart's true guide.

When I forget to give some love,
It sighs like a grumpy dove.
But quick to forgive, it stands so proud,
In funny poses, it'll draw a crowd.

A leaf or two might curl or fade,
But still it grows, it's unafraid.
With humor stitched in every vein,
It thrives on joy, not just on rain.

Embrace of Green Hearts

In bright green, the secrets grow,
Touch it gently, tiptoe slow.
It chuckles softly, with a jive,
A vibrant leaf, oh so alive!

This heart-shaped friend, a joyful tease,
Makes every worry simply freeze.
With spiky charms and hugs so tight,
It turns my frowns to pure delight.

At night, it dreams of sunny places,
While plotting ways to steal my aces.
In games of care, it wins with ease,
A champion in its leafy tease.

So let's toast with some plant-based cheer,
To every laugh, and every tear.
With love and joy, it bounces back,
An earthy spark, no humor lacks.

Healing Touch of Nature's Love

With a gentle touch, it starts to show,
A healing vibe, just like a pro.
It whispers softly in the night,
"Don't worry, friend, you'll be alright."

In moments dark, when shadows creep,
This leafy friend can help me leap.
With every gaze, it stays so bright,
Guiding me towards the light.

So take a seat, let's soak it in,
We'll laugh away the pangs and din.
With charming quirks and leafy grace,
You keep me grounded in this space.

Together, thriving, come what may,
This plant and I in funny play.
With nature's love, our spirits soar,
In every leaf, we find much more.

Love's Resilient Cradle

In the garden where giggles bloom,
Laughter dances, chasing gloom.
With prickly whispers from bright green friends,
Love's odd quirks, it never ends.

Hugs that are soft, with a twist of fun,
Heartfelt chuckles under the sun.
Silly moments, both sharp and sweet,
Where joy and hilarity love to meet.

A little sunshine, on the leaves it shines,
Spines and smiles, where joy intertwines.
Bounding laughter, a playful chase,
In this odd love, we've found our place.

So here's to the blooms that never complain,
Our quirky romance, forever in grain.
From the roots to the tips, we laugh out loud,
In our wacky garden, together we're proud.

Embracing Nature's Salve

Under the sun, with a wink and a grin,
Nurturing sweetness with a bit of sin.
A gentle touch, oh so absurd,
Nature's embrace, the silliest word.

With every petal, a ticklish cheer,
Tales of joy, whispered near.
Plants that giggle, just like we do,
Spreading smiles, both old and new.

Misfit buds in a whimsical clump,
Frolicking softly, each little bump.
So bring on the antics, win the day,
In this lively dance, we laugh and play.

With every bloom, a gentle tease,
Tickling hearts like a warm breeze.
Wrapped in giggles, forever we stay,
In nature's charm, we find our way.

Greenery's Gentle Promise

In a patch of green, where the punchlines sprout,
Life's little jokes are what it's about.
Leafy laughter fills the air,
With zany puns, there's love everywhere.

Whiskers of leaves, they tickle the sun,
In our goofy garden, we're never done.
Chasing shadows, chuckling bright,
Finding joy in every sight.

The vines entwine like our own quirky tale,
Silly treasures, love's fine detail.
Nature's whispers tickle the skin,
With every jest, our hearts begin.

So let the green marvel at our jest,
Together it seems, we're truly blessed.
In a patch of dreams, we plant our play,
With each blooming joke, forever we stay.

Sunlight and Shade in Harmony

In the dance of rays, where shadows meet,
Quirky mischief makes life so sweet.
Giggling plants under sunlit skies,
Laughter sprouting as joy never dies.

A sprinkle of shade adds to the fun,
With cheeky grins, we soak in the sun.
Sassy spines may stab and tease,
But it's all in good jest, if you please!

In the warm embrace, we wriggle and roll,
Nature's playground, where fun takes its toll.
Swirling in giggles, we dance and sway,
In our delightful garden, we found our way.

So let the rays shine and shadows prance,
In this silly love, let's take a chance.
With each playful jab, and every laugh,
In sunlight and shade, we find our path.

Cherished Growth in the Sunshine

In a pot so small and bright,
A plant with spines, a comedic sight.
It dances in the warm, soft light,
With every new leaf, it brings delight.

Watering can in a silly race,
I spill some here, it's all over the place.
My green friend wiggles, a bold embrace,
Thirsty giggles fill the garden space.

Sunshine kisses every cheek,
Who knew a plant could be so cheeky?
With every throb, it makes me peek,
At tiny blooms, it feels unique.

So here we stand, two pals in bloom,
One sharp, one soft, dispelling gloom.
In the garden's fun and busy room,
We laugh together, watching life zoom.

In the Company of Nature's Best

In the garden where laughter grows,
Surrounded by friends, each one knows.
A piebald bee with polka dot clothes,
Buzzing 'round, striking silly poses.

A chubby rabbit hops in glee,
With wiggly ears, oh what a spree!
Chasing butterflies, wild and free,
Nature's comedy, just wait and see.

Birds chirp secrets, a feathery crew,
Flapping about, they spread the news.
"Life's a stage, and we're all the views!"
A roguish tune, so light and blue.

So let's join in this cheerful mess,
With nature's laughs, we're truly blessed.
Life's funny moments we can't suppress,
In this green haven, we find our zest.

Sweet Petals and Spiky Sentiments

Among the petals sweet and wide,
Lurks a spiky friend with pride.
A jokester plant, it chides and glides,
Whispering tales of the wild side.

With every poke, it tells a tale,
Of love and laughter, without fail.
It giggles softly, not afraid to rail,
While I sip tea, tipping the scale.

In blossoms bright, the laughter leaps,
As nature's humor makes me weep.
So much joy, I can hardly keep,
Even the thorns have secrets deep.

So let us dance in this petal show,
With spiky pals putting on a glow.
In life's bouquet, let humor flow,
Together we'll watch the good times grow.

Love's Journey Through the Garden

In a garden where dreams take flight,
Two silly hearts dance in delight.
With spades and trowels, they plant the night,
Watering laughter, a joyful sight.

They stumble on weeds, their laughter loud,
With every fall, they feel so proud.
Nature giggles, as if endowed,
With whispers sweet, beneath the cloud.

Through petals bright, their love does twirl,
Swaying gently in a leafy whirl.
Caught by surprise in the garden's curl,
A reminder that life's a colorful pearl.

So here they roam, hand in hand,
Searching for joy, oh how it's planned!
In nature's arms, they take a stand,
A comical love in a whimsical land.

Soothe Me in the Shade

In the garden, we both sit,
With my plant that bites a bit.
You say it has a pointy style,
But it makes us laugh a while.

Sunshine glints upon your hair,
As you fuss with gentle care.
My prickly friend gives quite a scare,
Yet together, we've not a care.

In the breeze, the leaves do sway,
Tickling toes in a playful way.
We'll dance with thorns, just you and me,
Sipping lemonade happily.

With a wink and a cheerful grin,
Let's embrace the fun within.
While thorns may threaten our delight,
Laughter blooms under soft moonlight.

Prickly Yet Tender Caress

You said, 'Don't get too close, my dear,'
Yet here we are with giggles near.
With twinkling eyes, we jest and tease,
Sticking fingers in the breeze.

In danger, we find our sweet delight,
Jabbing blooms in the fading light.
Your laughter cracks the serious tone,
As nature gives us all its own.

Who knew that prickly things could shine?
With every poke, in jest, we dine.
You hold a leaf, I catch a thorn,
In this jest, new friendships are born.

So here's to fun in the flora's seat,
Together we face each prickly feat.
With smiles wide and hearts so bold,
Let's charm the thorns, and let love unfold.

Serene Gardens of Emotion

In this garden, laughter grows,
Among the petals, love bestows.
You say the green can be quite sly,
But all I offer is a sigh.

Every poke brings a playful sprout,
With a twist of fate, we laugh it out.
Your gentle voice, a soothing shade,
As we tease the leaves that never fade.

Upon my heart, a little sting,
Yet with your smile, I take to wing.
Every fear now replaced with charm,
In this garden, you're the calm.

So let's embrace what makes us grin,
Through the prickles, a beauty within.
Serene and silly, let's take a chance,
In this garden, let's laugh and dance.

Nature's Embrace Among Thorns

Underneath these thorny skies,
A natural mix of giggles and sighs.
With every poke, we draw in near,
A tender heart that knows no fear.

The sun shines bright on silky green,
In this wild and wacky scene.
You chase me round the prickly waves,
While the plant just quietly craves.

So here's to you, my kindred soul,
In the garden, we're on a roll.
Even thorns find their gentle ways,
Bringing laughter to our days.

Amidst the chaos, we find the bliss,
With every bump, there's love in this kiss.
So plant your heart near and dear,
In nature's embrace, we have no fear.

Breathing Life into Fond Memories

In the garden where laughter flows,
We dance like blooms in the summer glow.
You trip on vines with a comical grace,
A smile spreads wide on your sunny face.

In pots we keep secrets, tales yet untold,
With every tickle, our love unfolds.
Your hat flies off with a gust of the breeze,
We chase it together, oh, if you please!

Each leaf a story, each stem a jest,
We laugh at the quirks that we love best.
A sprout of mischief, a tickle of glee,
In this quirk-filled plot, just you and me.

So here's to the moments, both silly and sweet,
With you by my side, life's always a treat.
Let's plant our dreams in this quirky little spot,
For in our laughter, we have all we've sought.

In the Shade of Love's Garden

Under the branches, secrets we share,
You find a ladybug tangled in your hair.
With a giggle and grin, we make it our game,
In the shade of our laughter, nothing feels the same.

The garden's our stage, where antics unfold,
You pretend to be regal, yet your socks are bold.
A tumble, a giggle, as your crown tips away,
With every mishap, you brighten the day.

We wander through petals, all colors and hues,
Life's too short for mundane, we'll pick our own views.
With silly mishaps and playful debates,
In this thriving paradise, we embrace our fates.

So here's to the sunshine and silly little fights,
In the shade of this garden, let's share more delights.
With each bloom that blossoms, we're crafting our story,
A love that's absurd, yet forever in glory.

Sun-kissed Affection in Green

In the morning light, we giggle and chat,
You trip on a trowel, oh, imagine that!
With sun-kissed cheeks and blooms by our side,
Our love's a garden where laughter won't hide.

With fingers in soil, we dig up old dreams,
You toss me a daisy, or so it seems.
I splash in the fountain, a swoosh and a plop,
You watch wide-eyed, then laugh till you drop.

Each petal a giggle, every stem a delight,
Our antics unfold in the warmth of the light.
From sun-kissed mishaps to pollen dust fights,
We thrive in this garden with shared little flights.

So raise up your shovel, let's dig deep and wide,
For in this green sanctuary, we'll journey with pride.
Planting seeds of joy, we'll water with laughter,
In this sun-kissed affection, we are happily ever after.

Petal Soft Promises

With petals surrounding, we promise a dance,
You twirl like a flower, oh, take a chance!
A stumble, a giggle, you step on my toes,
But laughter's the rhythm, that's how love grows.

In the bloom of the moment, we joke and we tease,
With every sweet whisper, we do as we please.
You steal my hat and dash 'neath the trees,
I chase after you, our hearts at ease.

Our garden's a symphony, full of sweet notes,
Where petals and punchlines are what love promotes.
With each soft promise, we cultivate cheer,
In this petal-soft world, we have nothing to fear.

So let's laugh through the seasons, let joy be our creed,
With humor the water, and love as the seed.
In this playful romance, we find a sweet blend,
With petal soft promises, our laughter won't end.

www.ingramcontent.com/pod-product-compliance
Lightning Source LLC
Chambersburg PA
CBHW070323120526
44590CB00017B/2804